AF335159

ON THE MOVE...

Just about *Anything* Can Be Moved

By David Paige

CHILDRENS PRESS, CHICAGO

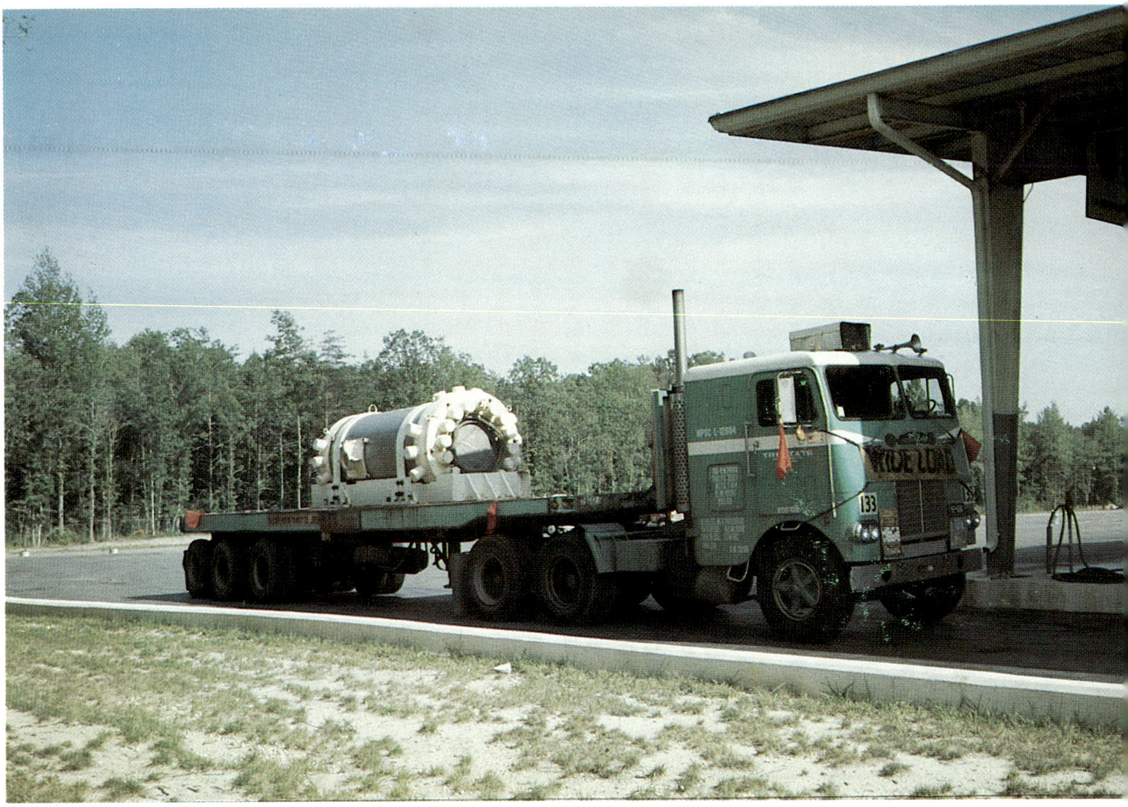

Moving used nuclear fuel

Library of Congress Cataloging in Publication Data

Just about anything can be moved.

(On the move)
SUMMARY: Briefly discusses the difficulties of moving hazardous cargoes and large objects, focusing on nuclear materials and the temples at Abu Simbel.
1. Moving of buildings, bridges, etc.—Juvenile literature. 2. Radioactive substances—Transportation—Juvenile literature. 3. Abu Sunbul, Egypt. Grand Temple of Ramses II—Juvenile literature. 4. Transportation—Juvenile literature. [1. Moving of buildings, bridges, etc. 2. Radioactive substances—Transportation. 3. Abu Sunbul, Egypt. 4. Transportation]
I. Title.
TH153.W47 629.04 80-22669
ISBN 0-516-03889-3

Printed in the United States of America.
1 2 3 4 5 6 7 8 9 10 R 89 88 87 86 85 84 83 82 81

Photographs courtesy of Tri-State Motor Transit Compa
UPI, 5, 9, 18, 27, 31; Wide World Photos, 6, 8, 23 (left),
38, 39; Consulate General of the Arab Republic of Egyp
13, 15, 34, 35; UNESCO/Keating, 17, 21, 23 (right, top a
bottom), 25; Shell Oil Company, 29, 32; United States N
36, 37; Temple Israel, 41, 42.
Front Cover; Two statues of Ramses II, Consulate Gener
of the Arab Republic of Egypt
Back cover; An oil tanker, Shell Oil Company

TRANSPORTING NUCLEAR MATERIAL

The sign on the large trailer truck or railroad car could say: "Caution—Nuclear Bomb Inside." But it won't. But there *is* nuclear material inside. It may be nuclear material that could be made into a bomb. But no one wants to tell you what is inside.

Moving dangerous materials is nothing new. In Chile, truck drivers for years have hauled nitroglycerin. This is highly explosive. It can blow up if the truck has a sudden, hard shock. The trucks drive over the most winding, bumpy mountain roads.

Highly explosive and poisonous materials are moved daily. They are carried by truck or railroad car. This happens everywhere.

   Underlined words are defined in the glossary at the back of the book.

Among the most dangerous things moved today is nuclear cargo. No one used to worry about shipping nuclear materials. That was before World War II. Atomic and nuclear power were not used for <u>energy</u> or <u>weapons</u> then. But the war and the development of the <u>atomic bomb</u> changed all that. We entered the <u>Nuclear Age.</u> Now moving nuclear materials is common. The military does it. Businesses do it.

There are many kinds of nuclear weapons now. They include bombs and <u>missile warheads.</u> They include other explosives. They are powerful and <u>destructive.</u> They are more powerful than the atomic bombs of World War II. Now a number of nations besides the United States have them.

Today there are many uses for nuclear energy. <u>Nuclear energy programs</u> are at work in 44 different countries. They are

A radiation containment chamber

on every continent in the world except
Antarctica. In the United States alone,
there are more than 70 nuclear power
plants presently in operation. Another
85 are in the process of being built. These
plants make electric power.

Mildly radioactive soil is placed in trenches awaiting burial.

Have you seen pictures of the great mushroom cloud from a <u>nuclear explosion</u>? Nuclear materials can be powerful. But explosion is not the danger in moving nuclear materials. These materials can be made into very destructive weapons. But they will not explode in a crash. They will not catch fire as gasoline or other chemicals could. There are, however, *two* very real dangers.

The first danger is the release, or leakage, of harmful radiation. Nuclear materials are radioactive. That is, they produce or give off radiation. You cannot see it. But the radiation can cause serious harm to humans. The radiation can attack and destroy cells in the body. It can possibly cause cancer or birth defects. It can create other health-related problems.

The other danger is someone hijacking a truck or railroad car carrying a nuclear weapon. Or someone might steal the nuclear materials that are being moved. The thief could be a terrorist or a criminal. This could result in a disaster.

Nuclear materials or weapons are moved from one place to another. But it is done very carefully. Nuclear weapons are moved from place to place by the U. S. government. Nuclear material used to

This railroad car moves used nuclear fuel.

make nuclear explosives—Uranium 235
and Plutonium—are also moved. The
government and the military call this
freight Special Nuclear Material (SNM).

The Army, Navy, Air Force, and
Marine Corps move SNM. The
government's Energy Research and
Development Administration (ERDA)
also moves SNM.

The nuclear power plants need nuclear
materials. They help to make electric
energy. The nuclear materials must be

Unlike many others carrying similar material, this truck *does* say radioactive.

shipped both to and from the plants. First, the materials must be brought to where they will be used. Secondly, the radioactive <u>waste</u> has to be taken away and dumped. This is usually in the ocean or underground. There are different kinds of radioactive wastes. They can be used-up fuel. They can be <u>nuclear pellets and rods.</u> They can be clothes or trash that have been exposed to radioactivity.

Nuclear materials must be handled with care. They can be very dangerous. They have to be well-protected.

MOVING THE TEMPLES AT ABU SIMBEL

In 1960 work was to begin on the Aswan High <u>Dam</u>. It is in Egypt. It was a big job. It would take more than 10 years to complete. It had to be done to control yearly flooding of the Nile River. The dam would give more farmland to Egypt and its neighbor to the south, the Sudan.

By building a dam, a 312-mile-long lake would be made. This would fill about 5,000 square miles with water.

There was a problem, however. This spot was rich in <u>archaeological</u> treasures. Many treasures would be flooded. So, in the 1950s, the governments of Egypt and the Sudan, along with the United Nations Educational, Scientific and Cultural Organization (UNESCO), set up a program. They decided to find and save any of the temples, tombs, or other artifacts of ancient Egypt that might be flooded.

During the next eight years, 70 groups were sent into the area. Hundreds of scientists, archaeologists, and engineers came. They began looking for relics to be saved. More than 600 important places were uncovered. They were beneath the shifting sands of the desert. Work got going immediately. They tried to save everything worthwhile.

The greatest problems were the temples at Abu Simbel. These super structures had been carved into a big sandstone cliff. This was along the west bank of the Nile River. They were more than 3000 years old.

The temples had been built for Ramses II, an Egyptian <u>pharoah</u>, and his queen Nefertari. This was around 1250 B.C. Ramses II was a <u>god king</u>. He had the temples built to honor himself and his queen. The temples also honored some of the Egyptian gods.

The larger of the two temples had four big statues of Ramses II. They were <u>sculpted</u> at the entrance. Each statue was 67 feet tall. The temple itself was 125 feet wide. It was 100 feet high. It went 200 feet back into the cliff. The inside of the temple had halls, one after another. The halls were carved out of the solid rock. Each was decorated with <u>sculptures.</u> There were also paintings on the walls.

The temple faced the east. Twice each year the first rays of the rising sun would shine through the entrance. The sun would travel the length of the halls. It would shine upon a statue of Ramses II and his fellow gods. They were 200 feet inside the temple.

The smaller temple was 90 feet wide. It was 40 feet high. It was cut 70 feet into the cliff. Ramses II <u>dedicated</u> it to Queen Nefertari. He had six statues carved into the face of the cliff at the entrance. Each statue was 33 feet tall.

The temples had great <u>historical</u> <u>value</u>. Also Greek and Phoenician soldiers arrived later. They carved their names on the front of the larger temple. It was the "<u>graffiti</u>" of ancient times. It helped us to study the early history of the alphabet.

The temples were very important. But the job of moving them was not going to be an easy one.

How could the temples be saved? All sorts of suggestions were made. One idea was to have each temple cut out in one large block. Then each would be raised to the top of the cliff. That would mean lifting each temple straight up the height of a 19-story building.

Another plan suggested the building of a great <u>pontoon.</u> On it the temples could be floated to another location. One idea was to cause a nuclear explosion that would reroute the Nile around the area of the temples.

By 1963 the time for saving the temples was running out. Still no plan had been agreed upon. Soon the rising Nile waters would flood the area.

Then a plan was accepted. It was the idea of some Swedish engineers. It called for cutting the temples into blocks. Each block would weigh about 20 to 30 tons. The blocks would be hauled, one at a time, up a road to the top of the cliff. Here the temples would then be rebuilt. The cost of the move was put at between $32 and $36 million. The job would be carried out

by a team of public works <u>contractors.</u>
They were from France, Germany, Italy,
Sweden, and Egypt. Actually, more than
50 nations helped with the move. They
helped with money, equipment, and/or
workers for the job.

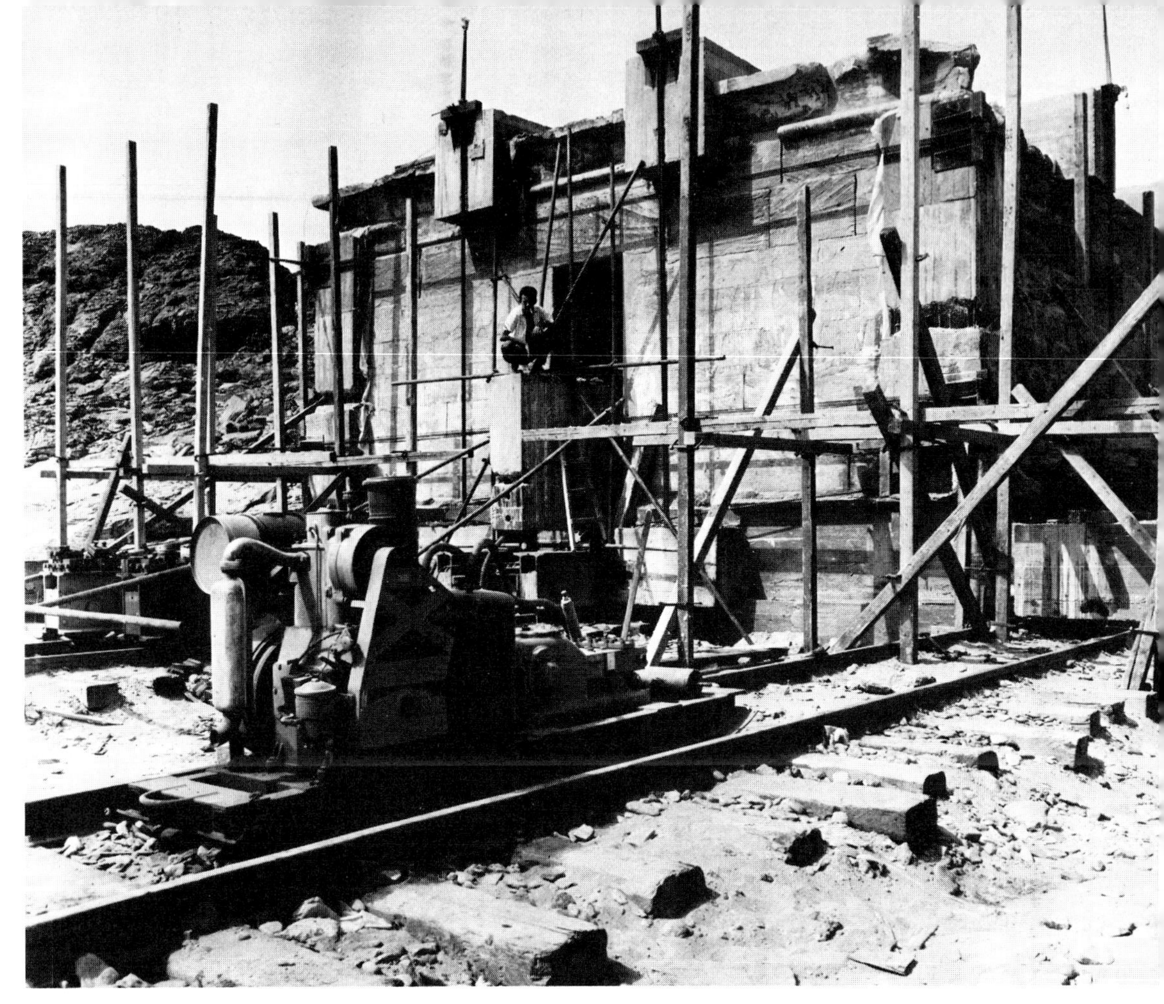

The plan called for three operations. First the cliff was dug out to <u>expose</u> the temples. This meant removing about 300,000 tons of rock.

Second, each temple was cut into blocks. They were then hauled to higher ground. The blocks were stored until all the blocks of the temples were removed.

Third and last, the temples were rebuilt. They were 210 feet higher. They were 590 feet farther inland from where the temples had first stood. They were also set in the same direction. They were facing the rising sun.

A crew of about 1,500 got to work. They were in a race against the waters that would soon flood the area. They worked seven days a week, 24 hours a day. They worked in three overlapping 12-hour shifts.

The first thing they did was to build what was called a "cofferdam." This held the water away from the temple. The cofferdam was built out from the cliff. Three drainage tunnels were dug. Pumps were installed. The pumps fed water into a drainage pipeline.

After the cofferdam was in place a new problem arose. Water began to ooze up from under the cofferdam. The temples might crumble if the water kept coming into the bottom. The engineers in charge flew in eight tons of <u>drilling rigs.</u> They dug 15 deep wells. Then 15 underwater pumps were installed. The pumps removed the water oozing in.

Sand—34,000 tons—was then piled against the front of the temples. This would cushion the front from falling rock. Chutes at either side of the temples were built. The material dug up was fed into the chutes. This fell down and filled the cofferdam.

Steel <u>scaffolding</u>, padded with felt, was set up in the rooms of the temples. This supported the ceiling and walls. Entrance to the temples could now only be gained through a large tube. This went through the protective layer of sand.

Pneumatic hammers, compressed air drills, rock chisels, and ripper tractors were used. They stripped the rock from around the temples.

Oscillographs were used. They could measure to see if the drills and tractor equipment were hurting the structure of the temples. As it turned out they were. So it became necessary to remove the last 60,000 tons of rock by hand. Then the temple was ready to be cut into blocks.

Tests were made on sandstone from other parts of the cliff. This helped decide the best way to cut the blocks and move them. Some of the sandstone broke easily. To make it stronger, a <u>synthetic resin</u> was forced into it. Stone hooks were made. They were sunk into the blocks with a synthetic resin <u>compound</u>. They were used as handles for raising the blocks.

Many kinds of cutting tools were also tested—disc saws, chain saws, and other handsaws. Finally, a special, diamond-toothed handsaw was made for the job.

The saws were used by the finest stonecutters from Italy's marble quarries. The stonecutters made their cuts. Then plastic resin was sprayed over the surface. This stopped the sandstone from crumbling. Each cut was under the watchful eye of an archaeologist. Tension was very great. One workman broke a tiny chip from a block. He burst into tears.

Each block was cut away. Then it was
lifted by a <u>derrick</u> onto a flat truck. The
truck had been loaded with sand for
cushioning. The truck moved slowly,

inches at a time. It went up a paved road built for this purpose. Each block received a protective covering at the storage area on top of the cliff. It was numbered so that its exact position in the temple would be known.

The work went on, block by block. Finally, the flooding waters washed over where the temples had stood. But the last block had just been lifted out and hauled away. It was a face of one of the statues of Ramses II.

In all, there had been 1,041 blocks. It was now April, 1966, three years after the beginning. Now the temples had to be rebuilt.

The blocks were put on scaffolding. Each block was fixed to or hung from a <u>reinforced concrete</u> supporting structure. <u>Concrete domes</u> were constructed on top of the supporting structure. Overlying rock was placed over the concrete domes. Next, the face of the temples was put in place.

The stonemasons reassembled the statues of Ramses II. They had to jam paper-thin pieces of stone into cracks. They had to fill up any holes.

By 1968 the great job was completed. Of all the 1,041 blocks, only 57 were damaged. Only two crumbled. They were replaced. The entire job took six years to complete. But the temples of Abu Simbel built so long ago were saved for the future.

AND A FEW OTHER MOVES

All kinds of things have to be moved at one time or another. Every day of the year, in fact, people pack up and move. Usually they leave their home where it is. They just move their belongings. But some have taken their house right along with them. They just cut it away from its foundation. They jack it up. They slide a flatbed trailer under it. Then they haul it off to a new location.

On land, moves are usually by truck. There are tank trucks and trailer trucks. There are double-trailer trucks and flatbed trucks. There are many smaller trucks for special moving jobs. The

ERNST MOVERS

biggest truck ever built is the Rotinoff
Tractor Super Atlantic. It was used to
transport huge parts of an atomic power
station in England. When fully loaded,
the Rotinoff has a total weight of 412 1/2
tons.

In the air, the largest mover, or cargo
plane, is the Guppy. The whole front of
the airplane opens like a giant door. Inside
there is 39,000 cubic feet of space. It
moved the third stage of the *Saturn V*
rocket. It was the only airplane large
enough.

But the largest movers are not trucks
or planes. They are sea-going <u>tankers</u>.
They are known as <u>supertankers</u>. The
largest of these are the three French
supertankers. They are the *Pierre
Guillaumat*, the *Bellamya*, and the *Batilus*.

The size of the ship is its total weight. This means the <u>cargo</u>, <u>stores</u>, and fuel that the ship can carry. This is called the ship's <u>deadweight tonnage</u>, or just dwt. There are more than 700 ships in the world today that are 200,000 deadweight tons.

Some superships are between 200,000
and 300,000 dwt. Each is called a Very
Large Crude Carrier (VLCC). Some are
over 300,000 dwt. These are Ultra Large
Crude Carriers (ULCC). The three
largest supertankers are very big. They
have deadweight tonnage of more than
550,000.

Let's get an idea of just how large these
three are. Imagine a ship longer than three
and a half football fields. It is almost one
and a half times as *wide* as a football field.
The *Pierre Guillaumat* and the *Bellamya*
are 1,359 feet long. The *Batilus* is one foot
shorter. All three are 206 feet wide.

In the water, the ships are like giant
icebergs. Their keels ride 94 feet below
the water's surface when they are loaded.
The decks are only 24 feet above the

GLOBTIK TOKYO

water. They can travel at speeds of about
16 1/2 <u>knots</u>. This is equal to about 19
miles per hour.

These tankers can carry a cargo of oil
worth more than $50 million.

These superships need a safe-water
depth of 95 feet or more. Many harbors are
not deep enough. Sometimes the

supertankers unload 50 miles or more from the shore. These great ships are almost always on the move. Supplies are often delivered by launch or helicopter. The crew spend most of the time on the high seas. They can go to movies aboard ship. They can swim in the ship's pool.

Supertankers are the largest single "movers" today on planet Earth. But moves do not have to be big to be exciting or interesting.

Part of the <u>King Tut</u> exhibit was moved from Egypt to the United States. It was not so large. But it was one of the most careful moves of all time. The items to be put on display were ancient, <u>fragile</u>, and priceless. They were made of the finest gold, silver, <u>alabaster</u>, <u>obsidian</u>, and <u>precious gems</u>. They were made during the great age of ancient Egypt. They could never be replaced.

It was the largest <u>exhibition</u> of artifacts
ever taken out of the museum at Cairo,
Egypt. It showed the solid gold mask of
King Tut. There were small pieces of wood
and glass. They had been <u>handcrafted</u> by
<u>artisans</u> several thousand years ago. Each
piece was packed separately with great

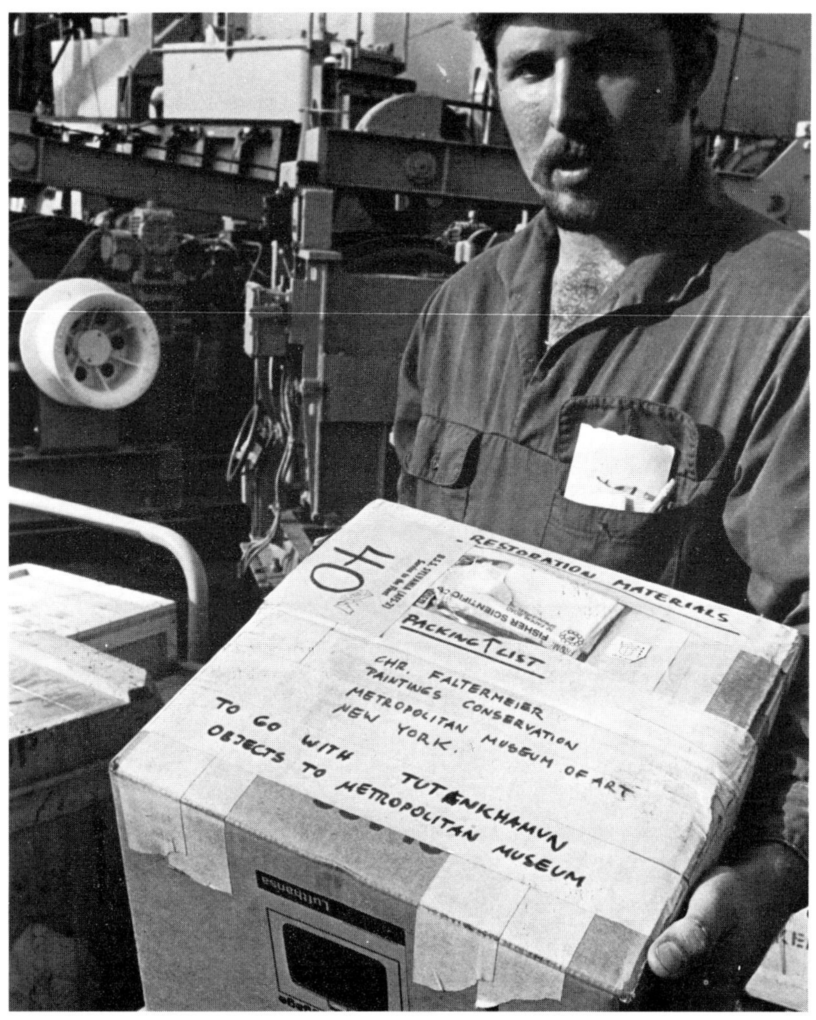

care. The items were then brought aboard
two ships. The ships were from the U. S.
Navy's Sixth Fleet. The pieces were <u>lashed</u>
to a special grilled-metal deck. They
would be safe even in the worst of ocean
storms. Humidity and temperature inside
the boxes was controlled.

NO SMOKING
USN

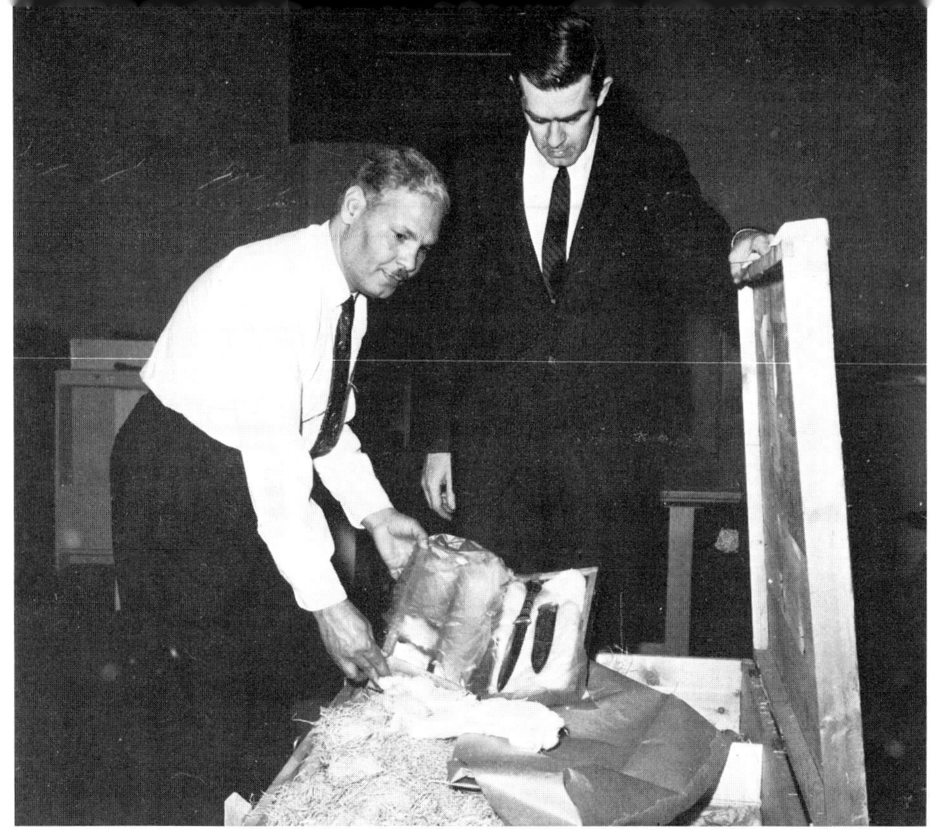

An art expert uncrates a case from the exhibit.

Once in the United States, the exhibit went to Washington, D. C. It went to other U. S. cities. Then it finally reached the Metropolitan Museum in New York City. Each time it was moved, each item had to be specially wrapped. Each item was packed separately. During each move, <u>security</u> was tight. Some things were kept secret. This was to protect the cargo.

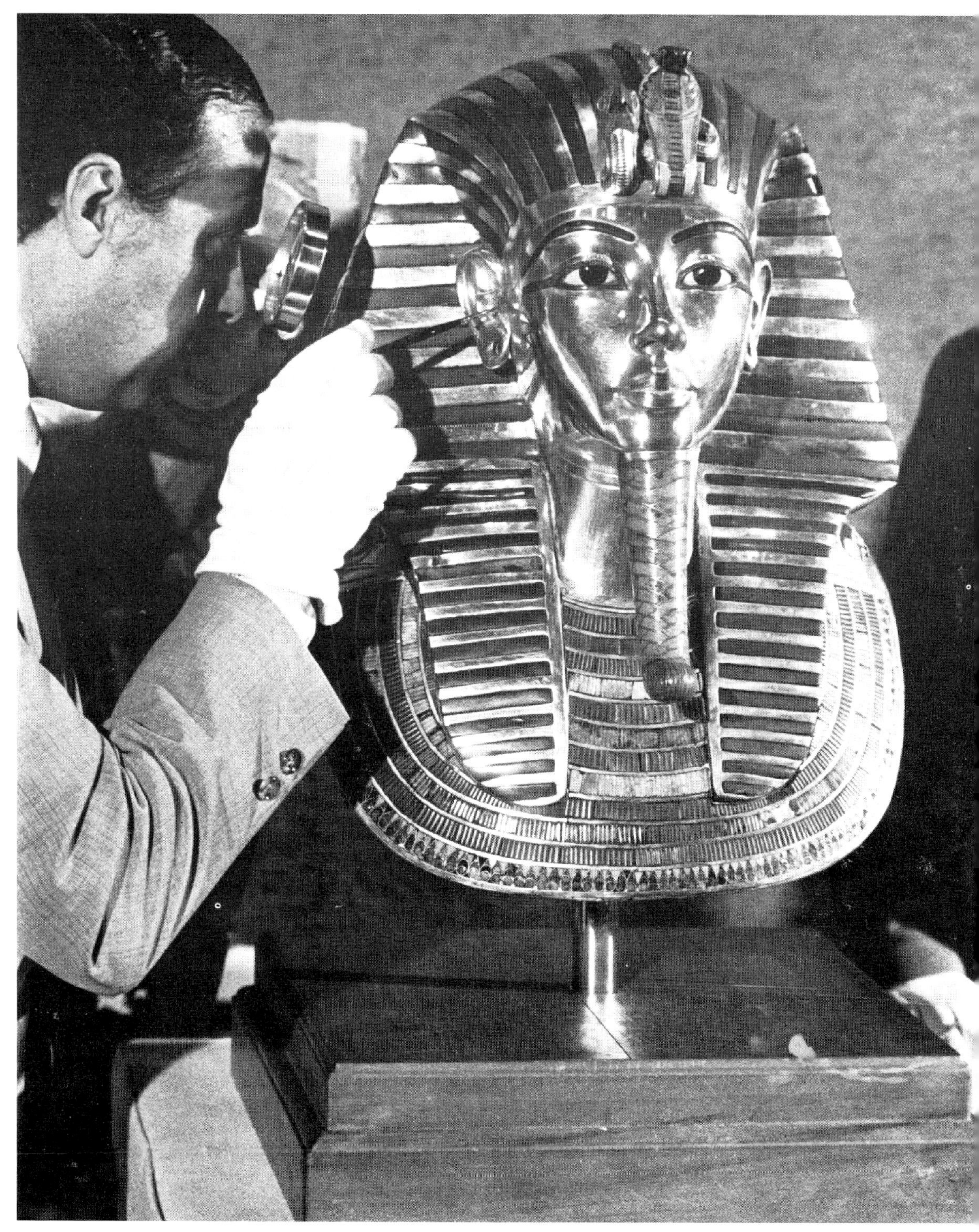

Inspecting the gold mask of Tutankhamun for possible damage

Then, there was the move the director of
the Lincoln Park Zoo in Chicago faced.
He had to travel to the island of Sri Lanka
in the Indian Ocean. Here he picked up a
baby elephant. He brought it back to the
zoo.

That was some job. He had to plan the
elephant's crate. The elephant was put in
the cargo section of the plane. That is
where suitcases or mail go. It was a long
plane ride back. The director had to go
down to the cargo section every so often.
He fed the elephant milk from a rather big
baby bottle.

And lastly, you might think that when
you die you go to your "final resting
place." But you might find that is just not
so.

When a dam is built, for example, it is
often necessary to move items from the
area. Otherwise they will be flooded.
Houses or buildings are often left where
they are. They become parts of underwater
ghost towns.

In 1967 Temple Israel in Dayton, Ohio, moved its cemetery to a new site.

But there are some things that people do not want flooded over. That could be a <u>cemetery</u>. People want to visit the <u>graves</u> of those who have died. So, they will have the cemetery moved. That involves a lot of things.

First a new <u>site</u> will have to be found nearby. The new land must be bought. Then people have to give permission to move the graves.

Each <u>coffin</u> must be dug up separately. Each must be labeled. Sometimes old coffins are damaged or destroyed. Then,

41

The old cemetery dated back to 1850. In the new cemetery, the original markers are arranged to give the appearance of an old cemetery.

the remains (the <u>skeleton</u>) must be carefully collected. It must be placed in a special plastic bag. It will then be moved to a new coffin. <u>Headstones</u> must also be moved. They are taken with the coffins to the new site. Each coffin is reburied. Each headstone or marker is reset.

So, it seems, just about everything, large or small, living or not living, is moved at one time or another.

GLOSSARY

Alabaster / 'al-ə-ˌbas-tər: a fine-grained mineral, often white, used for making ornamental objects

Ancient / 'ān-shənt: very old; of a time long past

Archaeological / ˌär-kē-ə-'läj-i-kəl: studying people and things of times past

Archaeologist / ˌär-kē-'äl-ə-jəst: someone who studies people and things of times past

Artifact / 'ärt-ə-ˌfakt: a man-made object such as a tool, weapon, or household article

Artisan / 'ärt-ə-zən: a person who is trained in arts and crafts; a craftsman

Atomic bomb / ə-'täm-ik 'bäm: an explosive weapon of great power

Birth defect / 'bərth 'dē-ˌfekt: to be born with a fault; to be imperfect when born

Cargo / 'kär-gō: freight carried by a ship, airplane, or other vehicle; a load

Cemetery / 'sem-ə-ˌter-e: a place to bury the dead; a graveyard

Chisel / 'chiz-əl: a metal tool with a sharp edge used to cut or shape wood or stone

Cofferdam / 'kȯ-fer-ˌdam: a temporary structure built to hold back water

Coffin / 'kȯ-fən: a box in which the dead are placed so they can be buried

Compound / 'käm-ˌpau̇nd: anything made up of two or more materials

Compressed air drill / kəm-'prest 'a(ə)r 'dril: a machine powered by air under great pressure; used to make holes

Concrete dome / 'kän-ˌkrēt 'dōm: a rounded, roof-like structure made of a mixture of cement, sand, gravel, and water

Contractor / 'kän-ˌtrak-tər: a person who builds or makes structures

Criminal / 'krim-ən-əl: a person guilty of a crime

Dam / 'dam: a wall built to hold back flowing water

Dangerous / 'dānj-(ə-)ras: unsafe; able to do harm

Deadweight tonnage / 'ded-'wāt 'tən-ij: the total weight of a vessel with everything in it

Dedicated / 'ded-i-ˌkāt-id: set aside for a special purpose; to honor a person or event

Derrick / 'der-ik: a large machine for lifting or moving heavy things

Destructive / di-'strək-tiv: breaking up; tearing down; spoiling

Disaster / diz-'as-tər: a happening that causes much damage or suffering, as a flood or earthquake

Drainage tunnel / 'drā-nij 'tən-ᵊl: a passage through which liquid can be made to flow away

Drilling rig / 'dril-in 'rig: equipment used to make holes deep into the ground

Energy / 'en-ər-jē: the power or force to do work

Engineer / 'en-jə-'ni(a)r: a person trained to work at planning and building roads, bridges, buildings, etc.

Exhibition / ˌek-sa-'bish-ən: a public display or showing

Explosive / ik-'splō-siv: a substance that can explode or blow up

Expose / ik-'spōz: to uncover; to let be seen

Flatbed trailer / ˌflat-ˌbed trā-lər: a large van with a flat, even top that is pulled by a truck or tractor

Foundation / faủn-'dā-shən: the base on which a structure rests

Fragile / 'fraj-əl: easily broken or damaged

God king / 'gäd kiŋ: a head of a country who also is considered like a supreme being

Graffiti / gra-'fēt-(ˌ)ē: words written on walls or sidewalks

Grave / 'grāv: a place in the ground where a dead body is buried

Handcrafted / 'hand-ˌkraf-təd: something made by hand and not by machine

Headstone / 'hed-ˌstōn: a marker made of stone set at a grave; gravestone

Hijacking / 'hī-ˌjak-iŋ: stealing something moving; stealing something from a moving vehicle

Historical value / his-'tȯr-i-kəl 'val-(ˌ)yü: something of worth that deals with past events

Iceberg / 'īs-ˌbərg: a large piece of floating ice that breaks off a glacier

Keel / 'kē(ə)l: the bottom of a ship or boat

King Tut / 'kiŋ 'tət: the person in 14th century B.C. who ruled Egypt

Knot / 'nät: a measure speed boats or ships use; equal to one water mile or 1.15 land miles per hour

Label / 'lā-bəl: a slip of paper on which information is written and attached to an object

Lashed / 'lasht: fastened with a rope; tied down

Leakage / 'lē-kij: seeping out; escaping through a crack or hole

Missile warhead / 'mis-əl 'wȯ(ə)r-ˌhed: the forward part of a weapon that has an explosive in it

Nitroglycerin / ˌnī-trə-'glis-(ə)rən: a highly explosive liquid used in making dynamite and other explosives

Nuclear / 'n(y)ü-klē-ər: having to do with the core of the atom

Nuclear Age / 'n(y)ü-klē-ər 'āj: the time in which we live since the use of atomic power

Nuclear energy programs / ˌn(y)ü-klē-ər 'en-ər-jē 'prō-grams: getting power from the rearrangement of certain parts of the atom

Nuclear explosion / 'n(y)ü-klē-ər ik-'splō-zhən: a powerful release of energy from the rearrangement of the core of the atom

Nuclear pellets and rods / 'n(y)ü-klē-ər 'pel-əts 'ən(d) 'räds: small balls and bars which are made of radioactive material and are used as fuel

Nuclear power plant / 'n(y)ü-klē-ər 'paů(-ə)r 'plant: place where electricity is generated with atomic energy being used as a fuel

Obsidian / əb-'sid-ē-ən: a type of rock which is a glass formed from lava from a volcano

Oscillograph / ä-'sil-ə-ˌgraf: a measuring instrument

Pharaoh / 'fe(ə)r-(ˌ)ō: the title of the rulers of ancient Egypt

Pneumatic hammer / n(y)ů-'mat-ik 'ham-ər: a machine powered by air pressure; used for pounding

Pontoon / pän-'tün: a boat with a flat bottom

Precious gem / 'presh-as 'jem: a stone of high value or worth

Radiation / ‚rād-ē-'ā-shən: the energy or rays sent out from atoms

Radioactive / ‚rād-ē-ō-'ak-tiv: gɪ̄: ing off energy in rays as a result of the breaking up of the atom's nucleus

Reinforced concrete / ‚rē-ən-'fō(ə)rst 'kan-‚krēt: a hard substance made of cement, sand, gravel, and water that is made stronger with steel bars or rods

Relic /'rel-ik: a thing or part of a thing that remains from the past

Ripper tractor / 'rip-ər 'trak-tər: powerful vehicles used to tear or pull apart

Scaffold / 'skaf-əld: a framework put up to support workers while they are working on something

Scientists / 'sī-ənt-əsts: persons who study things in science

Sculpted / 'skəlpt-id: carved or formed

Sculpture 'skəlp-chər: a figure made by carving or chiseling

Security / si-'kyu̇r-ət-ē: feeling safe; protected

Site / 'sīt: the place where something is or was

Skeleton / 'skel-ət-ᵊn: the framework of bones of a body

Stores / 'stō(ə)rs: supplies; cargo

Supertanker / ‚sü-pər-‚taŋ-kər: a very large ship used to move oil or other liquids

Synthetic resin / sin-'thet-ik 'rez-ᵊn: a sticky material made by putting chemicals together; man-made

Tanker / 'taŋ-kər: a vehicle used to move oil or other liquids

Temple / 'tem-pəl: a building for the worship of a god

Tension / 'ten-chən: nervous strain

Terrorist / 'ter-ər-əst: a person who uses force to make others obey or listen

Waste / 'wāst: matter left over or thrown out as useless; scrap

Weapon / 'wep-ən: a thing used for fighting

INDEX

ABOUT THE AUTHOR

David Paige is a former editor-in-chief for a book publisher who specialized in children's books. For the past seven years, he has devoted his time to fulltime writing. He lives in a suburb of Chicago with his wife and three children.